JEAN HARVEY

Chief Examiner of
The Associated Board of the Royal Schools of Music

Commentary on Piano Examination Pieces 1995

Grades 1–7

GW00691426

The Associated Board of the Royal Schools of Music

First published in 1994
The Associated Board of the Royal Schools of Music (Publishing) Ltd
14 Bedford Square, London WC1B 3JG

© 1994 by The Associated Board of the Royal Schools of Music

ISBN 1 85472 787 7

Printed in Great Britain by Caligraving Limited, Thetford, Norfolk

Commentary on Piano Examination Pieces 1995

Grades 1–7

Contents

2-95

Introduction

This year, for the first time, we are publishing in book form the commentaries included in the illustrated cassettes of the Piano Examination Pieces, Grades 1–7. Many teachers have found the recordings helpful and use them to supplement what is already being taught. It is hoped that teachers will also welcome the issuing of this booklet, as it provides easy reference to all of my commentaries to the pieces in Grades 1–7.

Firstly, let me discuss the purpose of these commentaries. It is not my intention to intrude between teacher and pupil, and the actual teaching of the notes I must leave to the teacher. At the same time, examiners hear many performances which consist of only the notes, and it is my intention here to suggest ways of thinking beyond this and building towards a more musical performance which will gain higher marks in our examinations.

The commentaries are shaped in part by the completed questionnaires and helpful letters which I have received from teachers. I have also used many opportunities to discuss with teachers what they wish to be illustrated and what I should say. While these commentaries are concerned with the pieces included in the examination syllabus, there are many general points which apply to a good deal of other piano music.

Please also look at the criteria for assessment published in my booklet *These Music Exams*. This shows, for each grade, what determines the Pass results and what we expect for Merit and Distinction. The added marks are given for evidence of actual *musicianship*, and this is why I stress style and structure over and over again. The booklet is free and available from most music shops; it also contains minimum suggested scale speeds.

I would like now to make a few general points before discussing the individual pieces in detail.

Thinking ahead

Firstly, it is essential to think forward all the time. To make anything musically shaped one has to focus ahead, even if only a few bars are involved. I am only too aware of the basic problems in learning notes,

1

when clumsy fingers refuse to become agile, and the triumph when one day the pupil is able to reach the end of a piece without breaking down. Perhaps a slow and cautious tempo is reached by the examination, and a few louds and softs may have been added, though without much understanding of why they are there. Yet it is only when the pupil is able to think beyond this that a musical performance will be possible.

When playing even the easiest piece, imagine reading a story, or watching a film, or painting a picture. In the story and film there will be character and plot, and both will work towards a climax. In the picture there will be foreground and background, but also a focal point; something will stand out — either a figure or a tree or a house — to draw your attention. Any piece of music must be created for the listener in the same way. We have the main tunes (the 'characters', if you like), what we do with them (the plot), and somewhere there must be a climax or focus to our playing.

Tempo

Many candidates play too slowly, and teachers find it unfair if low marks are given because of this, when everything else is generally correct. However, you must accept that adherence to the correct tempo can go a long way to bringing the music alive and to defining the character and style of the composition. Too slow a dance will not sound like a dance, and a light and elegant classical sonatina will lose all the sparkle if the passagework is slow and careful and has no flow. An imaginative piece will become very dull. Too slow a tempo in a romantic or lyrical piece will mean that the beats become vertical, and the phrases cannot move on or be expressive. If one wants to express happiness or excitement, one would most probably speak more quickly, and it is the same in music.

The tempo indications are there for good reason, not just at the whim of the editor. In these examinations we feel that we have a real responsibility in suggesting what will encourage the best performances at all grades. So although it is sometimes difficult to make children play quickly, it is a serious and necessary part of learning.

Rubato

Of all the elements we can use to make playing musical, *rubato* is by far the most effective, yet it is the most misunderstood and misjudged. The meaning is flexibility, elasticity, giving and taking, but so often all we hear is *taking*, and the balance is lost. This moving on and moving back is essential from the easiest pieces to the most difficult, and all good players if they are fine musicians use some form of *rubato*, albeit unconsciously, in every phrase that they play.

The most important point to remember is that the giving and taking must exist within a certain time limit, and that is usually within a phrase. Every phrase must have some form of rhythmic shape. Throughout my commentaries I should keep reminding you to find the main peak in each phrase, in each section, or even in the whole piece itself, and I shall repeat that we should move forward towards that peak via dynamics or tempo and then come down in dynamics or pull back to balance rhythmic shape.

In classical styles the measure of movement must be very slight and *accelerando* is too violent for what is needed. In romantic pieces be sure to pick up the original tempo again after slowing down. Too often, the only form of *rubato* used is a retarding at each phrase-end with a gradual slowing down of all vitality and momentum.

Scales

There is no better way to produce facility, speed, fluency, agility, and strong yet sensitive fingers than to practise scales, broken chords and arpeggios, and we include them in the examinations for this reason. All of us have favourite methods of limbering up — some use studies, some use exercises — but for pupils at the early stages of learning to play, scales are essential.

They teach so much. They draw attention to unwanted accents and dubious thumb-turns; they create hand positions which are to be found in much classical music; and arpeggios are without equal in getting us around the keyboard.

In pieces, co-ordination is often poor if the hands have to move together, and frequently a good performance falters as soon as quick co-ordination is required. So the co-ordination derived from practising scales and arpeggios is invaluable, particularly if they are practised rhythmically.

Scales and arpeggios need to be used in many different ways. Different rhythms and contrary motions are especially helpful. Candidates should not look at the keyboard when they play in contrary motion: it is just not possible to look at both hands at the same time!

Wrists are often not used properly when the thumb turns, especially when playing arpeggios, and there is too much elbow movement, which results in accents or a break in continuity. Lateral wrist movement can be taught from the preparatory test level, and this will save time later.

Broken chords are invaluable in unlocking stiff joints and the knuckles of the fingers. *Staccato* and *legato* should be encouraged as early as possible and not be just another obstacle to overcome when the syllabus requires it. Encourage practice with different dynamics in each hand when playing together. Once the notes are mastered this will help independence, and apart from anything else a *crescendo* to the top and a *diminuendo* downwards will create a shapely scale and arpeggio, particularly if the tempo is flowing. Use well-known scales to teach basic *cantabile* at a slow tempo, so that the pupil has time to think about what is happening to the arm, wrist and fingers when weight is applied through a supported wrist.

When scales and arpeggios are played too slowly, accents appear on every note; when they are played too quickly, clarity of articulation is lost. Finger touch is all that is needed for a fluent and shapely scale, while finger strength will produce well-articulated scales, and leads to the lightly detached touch used in the music of Bach, Scarlatti and other composers of the baroque period.

If only scales could be used to teach such basic principles as touch and tone, *staccato* and *legato*, *forte* and *piano*, then much of what has to be learned at a later stage, when there are more difficult pieces to play, will already feel natural.

Pedalling

Many candidates have real problems in trying to co-ordinate the foot and hands, especially in *legato* pedalling. Please remember that only the toes and front sole are really needed to use the pedal quickly. I say this because one sees many candidates lift the entire leg, which is too heavy to be used with agility, and this will lead to serious tension in the muscles. As with scale practice, good pedalling should be encouraged from the start so that it feels natural at later stages when the music becomes more difficult.

Editions

I must mention these, as I am aware from both the teacher seminars and the letters we receive that this is an issue which causes concern.

We could publish copies which have no editorial suggestions, especially of early music; but then teachers would ask why the examiners have said that the playing lacked colour or interest if there were no dynamics or phrasing indicated. Many composers of the baroque and early classical period were haphazard in their markings of dynamics or points of articulation, often not adding them at all. Our intention is to present an edition with these added by the editor in a way consistent with good performance practice and which will lead to stylish playing. The editor's suggestions are there to be of help and guidance, and for the young or inexperienced teacher it is wise to follow them. At Grade 8, where a piece is not published by the Associated Board, it is advisable to use one of the several good critical editions currently available.

In addition to those marks added by the editor, a good rule to follow is to rise and fall in dynamics with the rise and fall in pitch. This can usually be applied to both baroque- and classical-style pieces. Remember that we have two ways of creating interest when we play: the sensitive use of both dynamics and articulation, which we can use separately or together.

There is often confusion as to what constitutes a phrase, and examiners often listen to disjointed playing, with on-going lines broken by small slurs, accents and gaps. It is important to think in long phrases or sections and view the small slurs as points of articulation within a longer phrase which allow the music to breathe and come alive. Throughout the commentaries I will give as much detailed help as I can to show what I mean.

Finally, here is a short list of points which may be of value to you and your pupils.

• Consider starting with scales, so that the piano can be tested for touch.
• Choose the best pieces for pupils to play in an examination, by which I mean those that will show off the best features of their playing. Very often we hear batches of candidates all playing the same list, some quite unsuitably.
• Either play from the copy or from memory. There are too many examples of halting because of a memory lapse, with candidates then having to find their place in the music again.
• Encourage pupils to look ahead *before* the end of the line; many performances stop or hesitate here, and physical and mental preparation is vital for the music ahead.

- If ornaments are holding up the basic pulse, it is better to put in an easier option, or even miss them out altogether, as fluctuating rhythm is automatically penalised.
- Let your pupils become aware of what a good *forte* should sound like. Let them tell you which is better — a hard and strident sound, or a full, warm and unpercussive one.
- Remember that *rubato* does not only mean getting slower; one must pay it back by going that much faster as well.
- We do not usually hear repeats, but we *do* hear *Da Capo*s and *Dal Segno*s.
- Let pupils play in front of each other as often as possible, as this will eventually help them control anxiety and nerves.
- Keep the Board's published criteria in mind when you do your own assessments of your pupils prior to an examination. However, try to remain uninvolved and do not imagine the playing to be better than it is.

Grade 1

A:1 Anon. *A Toy*

This bright and happy piece is written in 4-bar sections, except for the last 8 bars, which should be thought of as one phrase. The main motif, the falling 5-finger pattern, comes in both hands and should be brought out quite crisply and strongly. Each 4-bar phrase should go towards the 4th bar, and the other hand should support any dynamics. The strongest part of the piece lies in bars 13 and 14, but remember that in this type of music the *forte* must not sound percussive.

Staccato notes should be light and short but must not be accented, and this is especially important at the end of slurs with quavers, as the 3rd beat is the quietest of the 3. The quavers should be articulate and even and steady, and remember to look ahead immediately afterwards, as the hand position changes.

Remember to think about placing the LH and RH thumbs on black notes in bars 11 and 12. When this piece was set before there was hesitation in these bars, and candidates also took an extra beat at the end of bars 4, 8 and 12. The rhythm was inclined to be unsteady as well in bars 17, 18 and 19, so careful counting is necessary.

A:2 Schumann *Melody*

Whenever we have included this piece in the syllabus, it has always been very popular, with its fine melody and gentle accompaniment. It is also very singable, and this always helps in thinking of the phrase shape.

The suggested tempo will keep it moving onwards, as it must not sound laboured with 4 beats in the bar. In the first line the phrases are 2 bars long; then there is one of 8 bars, which is repeated.

If you rise and fall in dynamics with the rise and fall in pitch, this will help to give shape to the phrases. For example, go towards the 3rd bar with a slight *crescendo* and die away in the 4th; then up again to a strong A in bar 7 and down as indicated. I think that the 4th line should have the stronger *crescendo*, and it will make the ending more effective if it is very quiet. But this is *your* choice.

Technically, even and steady fingers will be needed for the accompaniment, with sufficient sensitivity of touch to support the RH dynamics. If the hand seems stiff, then a slight rotary movement will help to relax tension.

Bars which may need isolated study are 4, 8, 11 and 12, and it may help to practise these bars in chords, to feel the changing thumb and hand positions. Some fingering indications may be difficult for any size of hand. Bar 8, for instance, where it is awkward to hold the F in the melody so that it goes down to the D smoothly; and bar 11, with the tricky twist from 3 to 4. There is almost bound to be a break in *legato* here, so I would suggest 5–4–3–2 in the top line of bar 11, with two thumb notes below, and 1–5–1–3 in the next bar.

Finally, what I might anticipate going wrong would be playing with too loud an accompaniment or with 4 solid beats in the bar, so be on your guard against these faults.

A:3 Petr Eben *The horses are grazing*

This is clearly divided into two very different sections, and I am sure that a story can readily be imagined from the title — perhaps the horses graze peacefully in the first part and then are surprised by something and gallop off in the second. The phrase lengths are interesting: 3 bars and 7 bars, then the more predictable 4 + 4.

The RH has the melodic interest in the first two lines and this is then handed over to the LH in the *più mosso* section. Here, *staccato* notes may be played with finger movement or hand weight, but whatever is chosen the tempo must not become slow. Dynamics can be strong — especially in the accents and the final *crescendo* to the *sforzando* ending — and should be well contrasted throughout.

Technically, remember to let the notes up before repeating them. Indeed, before the start of the examination, this could be what you try out on the piano, as the action varies on each instrument.

When practising this piece, try to sing the *legato* line in the first section: it needs a *cantabile* touch, so try to encourage an overlap of weight between the fingers (this type of *legato* may as well be taught at this stage when the notes are relatively simple).

Examiners will listen for a good *cantabile* sound with balanced dynamics in both hands, and excitement in the second half with clearly repeated notes and crisp *staccato*.

B:1 J.C. Bach *Aria in A minor*

The title suggests a song, and this should be kept in mind when shaping the melody into phrase lengths. Although there are many small slurs which should have articulation, there must be no accents to disturb the onward moving line of melody.

There should be a break at the commas, but each 8-bar section should be shaped in one long phrase, as the LH quavers indicate on-going movement. It is important to point this out because one listens to many performances where each small slur has an accent and a *staccato* ending, and of course one would never sing a melody in this way. However, the LH crotchets should be detached throughout, apart from bar 7; they should sound like bowing strokes, which would be light and clearly defined.

Apart from the simple *piano* and *mezzoforte* indicated by the editor, rise and fall in volume with the rise and fall of pitch. For instance, crescendo to the 3rd bar and diminuendo in the 4th; rise again to the 6th and fall to the double bar. Whatever you do, remember that this music is essentially gentle, so use only a limited range of volume.

Any difficulties will arise from poor co-ordination of the hands, or in finding larger intervals outside the 5-finger span — see, for instance, the RH in bars 3–4 and 11–12. Incidentally, the semiquavers in bar 12 should not sound like triplets, which would be a predictable error.

I have only one suggestion for the fingering which may be easier: at the end of bar 7, I think that 3–1 may fall more reliably than 4–1, and I would then use 2/4 for the next chord.

The choice of whether to play *legato* or with articulated slurs and detached notes must rest with you. In the early grades, the decision will depend upon the pupil's quickness of mind and agility of fingers, and, if they are genuinely confused by the independence required in the hands, then a smoother line may have to be chosen. However, what the editor has suggested will give a far better stylistic effect.

B:2 Gurlitt *Andantino in F*

With a *cantabile* melody and flexible supporting accompaniment this is similar to Schumann's Melody (A:2). It has clearly defined chords in bars 7–8 to show the end of the first phrase. Although the next phrase might stop at bar 16, it overlaps into the return of the first theme, and so the phrase beginning at bar 9 must be structured through to the end. All that is required is a slight *rallentando* at the overlap, but if you do this then play the final bars in time.

The dynamics are clearly marked, and I think that the peak overall should be in bar 12 (but only *mezzoforte*, as the character of the piece is very gentle).

The LH octave stretch in bar 4 will present technical problems — the 5th finger needs quick downward movement when the thumb plays the top C. I think that it would be helpful first to practise the LH in chords throughout to get the feel of the hand positions, taking especial care in moving the thumb to a black note in the 7th and penultimate bar. Incidentally, it would not be possible to play this piece unless the LH can stretch a 7th, and this may influence your choice of List A or B.

A final reminder: let the music breathe when there are rests, as very often they are ignored. Problems I would expect in the examination are hesitations at bars 4 and 7 (and again later at the repeat), and too loud an accompaniment.

B:3 Michael Jacques *Itchy Fingers*

Like A:3, this has quick changes of *legato* and *staccato* touch, melodies in both hands and vivid dynamics.

The tempo is very important here, as it should be restless and busy and unable to settle down. The peak of the whole piece is the *fortissimo* at the end, so think of what is to come when you reach the *forte* in bar 7.

Remember that a good *crescendo* is made up of the gradual increase of sound of each note — not just a series of accents; and in this piece especially, use *all* the quavers in the final *crescendo*.

The piece falls into two sections; one of 7 bars long, and then a further 8. Try to make a difference between the *staccato* notes, which should be crisp, and the heavy lined notes in bar 7. The accented chords at the end can be as loud as you like, and of course, bring out the LH in bars 4 and 5.

First Alternative E. Horák *Cuckoo*

This is very attractive and imaginative and is probably easier to play than A:3 or B:3. There are two ideas here, and I like to think of a cuckoo calling as it perches in a tree, then flying on when there is a flowing, gliding melody, then stopping again, and so on. Structurally, you may like to think in 4-bar phrases, but let the phrase beginning in bar 5 go through to the double bar.

The hand positions are straightforward and can initially be practised in chords, but with a very small hand the 7ths in bars 6 and 26 will only be possible if there is a lateral wrist movement to help. It is worth acquiring this flexibility at this early stage since it will be used as the grades rise, not least in thumb turns in scales and arpeggios.

Initially a crisp *staccato* will be needed, then both hands become *legato* until the second half where independence of hands will be required to produce *staccato* and *legato* in both parts.

The suggested dynamics will give interest, and if you want to do something in the second line, then I suggest that there is a small rise in volume to bar 9 and a *diminuendo* back to the double bar. Obviously, the last 4 bars should be the climax of the piece.

Examiners will listen for the LH changing in the second half to bar-long slurs, and a balanced accompaniment which will support good dynamics. Possible faults may be cutting short the rests on the 2nd beat, and lifting off the minims too soon.

Second Alternative
Gordon Jacob *Lullaby for a Chinese Infant*

This is written very simply, with its repetition of an 8-bar melody. This needs small breathing spaces but must be shaped into an 8-bar length. The rise and fall in dynamics will help and should, of course, occur in both hands, wherever the melody lies. This applies equally to the *pianissimo* in the second line, which should rise a little to help emphasise the lined or *tenuto* D in the LH — but obviously, these 8 bars in the LH must be extremely quiet.

It is important to think of a gentle, swinging rhythm which never actually stops from the quavers in bar 8 until the chords at the end.

Hand positions will have to be worked out in bar 16 and also in 20 and 22, and remember to join the E to the G in bars 25 and 26 while holding the tie.

Examiners will listen for sensitivity of dynamics, as the range is entirely *piano* and *pianissimo* and this is quite difficult to control.

11

Grade 2

A:1 J.S. Bach (attrib.) *Menuet in D Minor*

This is an attractive dance movement, as it not only has the poise and elegance of a minuet but is lyrical as well. It is worthwhile explaining to pupils the essential characteristics of a minuet — that is, a heavier first beat and a lightened 3rd beat.

The LH notes need separation, and crotchets must be detached, like bowing strokes. Also, lined notes should be held for their full lengths. The editor has suggested small articulation slurs in the RH and these will give added interest; however, be careful not to place accents on the beginning of the small slurs or on the *staccato* notes at the end, as this would interrupt the shape of the overall phrase. If you prefer your own interpretation, just make certain that it sounds stylistically acceptable. For my preference I think I would like to slur the 9th and 10th bars and the 11th and 12th bars together.

Think of dynamics rising and falling with the pitch, and this will also help to give structure to the sections. For instance, starting with *mezzo-forte*, make a *diminuendo* down to the 4th bar, then go up again to the 6th bar, and die away to the 8th. The second section is brighter as it is higher in pitch, but remember that *forte* tone must not be hard and strident in this type of music.

Technically there are some awkward passages, and it will be necessary to look ahead and prepare for different hand positions and large leaps. It is essential that hands can work independently, so that one can look at the keyboard to help find notes. When this piece was previously set, examiners heard large gaps in the pulse in bars 9 and 11 and also much stumbling in bars 13 and 14. Make certain that the RH thumb is prepared ahead for the C♯ in bar 14, as previously it played a white note; also look at the keyboard to help find the LH thumb D in the final bar. Remember also to count the double semiquaver-quaver pattern: this was another common mistake, with these groups usually played as triplets.

A:2 Reinecke *Song*

The melody line of this will demand quite a flexible hand movement, and lateral wrist movement will help play the larger intervals smoothly. Certainly, examiners will listen for a good *cantabile* tone quality.

There should be a small peak in each phrase, and this has been indicated in the first two phrases. However, the new phrase starting in bar 8 must be taken right through with increasing dynamics to the *forte* in bar 12, and this phrase does not end until the return of the original melody in bar 14. The accompaniment must support this *crescendo* of course, though without over-balancing the melody; it should cause no problems except for placing the C# in bar 11 and getting around the notes in 13 and 14. Obviously, it would be wise to practise these notes in chords to feel the intervals.

The last 4 bars are merely an extension of the theme, so do not make them slower, as the notes are already longer in length. It would be a good idea to count steadily here, as so often in examinations rests and longer note values are cut short.

A:3 Jenö Takács *Dialogue*

The title means 'talking', and the hands between them must try to give an impression of this.

The first two bars in the RH contain the theme, and whenever any part of this occurs it ought to be brought out. For example the LH echoes it at the beginning, while the order is reversed in bars 13–15. Make sure that the lined notes are held for their full length, even though they are repeated. As with all repetition, the notes need to go forward to a focal point — here the second bar of the theme.

The piece falls into two sections, with the second section starting at bar 13. The *più lento* bars are merely an extension of the first half, but remember to bring out the top notes in the LH as they have fallen a semitone from the previous bar. The strongest section must lie in bars 13–15 as although there has been a *mezzoforte* before, this time it is marked *espressivo* as well.

Count carefully, so that dotted crotchets and minims are not cut short. In the last 4 bars, regard the LH dotted minims as a gradual *diminuendo*, and listen carefully to how quiet they have become by the penultimate bar.

B:1 Mozart *Andante in E flat*

This piece has not been set before in the syllabus, and I think that it will appeal to many candidates. The only drawback is that B:2 demands good hand interplay, so it will depend upon individual pupils' weaknesses and strengths as to which list is presented for examination.

This piece requires a good lyrical tone quality, the ability to create long phrases which have many small articulation slurs and an awareness of balance and support in the LH. The notes themselves are simple to play, so musicianship is what will be assessed by the examiner.

By all means break up the phrases as suggested by the slurs, but remember to increase each small *crescendo* so that one is led forward to the 4th bar, thus creating a 4-bar phrase. In the third line, do the opposite, starting more brightly and strongly and come down to *piano* by the end of the line. You will then have created five phrases in all, but the really distinctive performance will have only three sections — that is, ending at each double bar-line. A slight *rallentando* can emphasise the ending.

One fingering suggestion may be helpful: that is to use 4–3–2 in the LH in the 4th bar, thus saving a thumb note on the B♭.

B:2 Czerny *Study in B minor*

The title is inclined to put candidates off, as it suggests a dull, boring exercise, but studies can often be disguised as attractive pieces and this one is a good example.

Even and steady hand interplay is a real technical skill and it is useful to have a piece in the lists which draws attention to this problem. The most common fault is to hear the notes isolated and rushed with a gap between each hand.

Obviously, the first task is to learn the notes, and it would be wise to play these in chords to find the hand positions. This is important as you will find that the hands collide, since they have to play the same note, common to both chords. Release the top note in the LH quickly, so that it can be repeated by the RH.

You may find the use of both thumbs awkward and clumsy, but there is really no alternative, as using the 2nd fingers cannot be consistent. Because of the black notes, the hands must be positioned over and into the black keys and this is another good technical exercise, as many pupils use only the edge of the white keys.

It will be wise to learn this with a slow quaver beat, listening carefully to the steadiness of the interplay, and only increase the metronome speed when this interplay is really reliable. If it goes wrong, slow it down. Eventually, of course, it must sound in crotchets, and I suggest that when you have mastered 120 as the quaver beat, put the metronome to 60 and think in crotchets. *That* is when the piece will start to become musical.

Another hint is to use different rhythms, and putting accents on the RH instead of the LH will force the hands to become independent of the written pulse.

If there is tension in the hands, then use a slight rotary movement to help. This is also useful as the melody line can be defined by stronger fingers with the slight hand weight behind them.

The piece is in two 8-bar sections which run into each other. Shape each with dynamics in both hands, the peak of the first half coming in the 6th bar, that of the second in the 14th. Rise and fall in volume with the melody line to give added interest. Also, make a slight *rallentando* in bar 8 to define the return to the opening.

A couple of fingering suggestions may be helpful. In bars 8 and 15, I would use 2–4 in the RH throughout, and in the last bar 5–3 instead of 4–1 in the LH.

B:3 Simone Plé *The Shepherd's Song*

If pupils prefer a melody and conventional harmonies then choose this piece instead of A:3.

A good *cantabile* is essential, and take care not to accent any of the small slurs, as this would break the line of the phrase. A firm sense of pulse is also very important, as although this is a flexible piece, which could easily be played on a flute or recorder, the rhythmic values must be counted precisely. Otherwise, I can foresee problems similar to those we encountered when the piece was in the syllabus before: cutting short minims and dotted minims, and fluctuations of tempo when the semiquavers occurred, with the semiquavers played too slowly or rushed together.

There are three sections: the first to bar 12, then to the end of the minor section at bar 22, and then to the end. Remember to bring out the melody when it falls in the LH and play the RH chords very quietly. (Another common fault in examinations is playing an accompanying RH too loudly.)

15

Dynamics, which are generally very quiet throughout, can rise a little from the soft start to the G in the 3rd bar and should then die away in the second line. I would bring up the volume slightly in bars 13–16, as this will emphasise the move to the minor key. Keep in mind that stronger tone should still be warm and singing, as there is no place for harshness in this gentle song.

First Alternative Weber *Ecossaise in G*

This is gentle and tender, and the only problems will arise in keeping this atmosphere when the ornaments occur in the second half. Note that these are *turns*, and should not be played as an even 5, or divided into 3 and 2 and played with the two LH quavers.

Another problem in this section will be moving the RH over the LH: make sure that the LH wrist is held low to avoid collision. It would probably be wise to memorise bars 18 and 19.

Apart from these points, the notes are not difficult to play, except to define the syncopation, slurs and *staccato* notes in the first section and to observe the dynamics. I think that the editor was right to insert two continuation bars which more clearly suggest only two sections instead of four phrase-lengths.

Second Alternative
Sandré *You can't catch me!*

This is fun to play and requires neat finger agility and facility in getting around the keyboard. Keep the fingers well controlled, and do not rush in the semiquaver groups. In the fourth line, lean towards the top register, and then come back to a normal position.

Careful counting will be needed in bars 7 and 8 to put the triplet in correctly and to avoid playing the *next* group as another triplet. The grace-notes from bar 9 should be very quick and can first be practised together with the next note; eventually, of course, they must be played before the beat. As the piece is very light-hearted, the *sforzando*s should not be too strong.

The hand size may determine whether this piece can be played, as the chords of a 7th may be too difficult with a limited span in the LH.

Grade 3

A:1 Handel *Air in B flat*

This piece demands good independence of hands, so if this presents a problem it may be better to use B:1 for examination purposes. It must flow well, and, although it has many slurs and some *staccato* notes, it should sound in two long phrases — one to the double bar and from there to the end.

Each section can be shaped by attention to the rising and falling semi-quavers to make points of interest, and the reliable rule of parallel rising and falling dynamics should be used. For instance, start brightly and come down to the 4th bar, then rise as suggested to the *forte* in bar 9. The quietest part of the second section should be at the trill, so that you can rise to a strong ending. This rise and fall in volume will help bring out the imitation. Listen carefully to ensure there will not be a series of accents on each new bar.

The *staccato* notes must be detached from the previous beat; I mention this because we often hear such notes slurred from the previous note, or slurred into the next bar, and this is not correct stylistically. The quavers in the LH which are not slurred can be played smoothly or detached: I think that the separated version would give a better effect. Be careful also to bring out the hemiola cross-rhythm in bars 10 and 11, and 18 and 19.

A:2 Beethoven *Sonatina in F, first movement*

This has all the stylistic ingredients of a classical movement, and is fun to play and cheerful and light-hearted in character. Good articulation, even passagework and crisp co-ordination are required to play it well, and if pupils have problems with the technical control of passagework, the 'waltz' by Gurlitt (B:2) may suit them better.

The form itself is unusual in that the first theme does not reappear at all in the recapitulation. Instead, the second theme (bar 8) takes its place at the start of the recapitulation (bar 50) and is used in the dominant preparation leading up to this. The more lyrical material first heard in the development is used again in what could be called the coda from bar 60 to the end.

One must use a bright and wide dynamic range, but remember that *forte* tone should not be hard or accented. Even the final chords should be quick and crisp rather than just heavy.

I think that the strongest part of the first section should begin at the *forte* in the 5th bar, though the listener should feel that the whole of the opening three lines lead to the double bar.

In the middle section the alternating *fortes* and *pianos* will give lots of interest, but when the *crescendo* begins in bar 34, try to think of it going right through to bar 43, and, of course, the LH must help in supporting the RH. This *crescendo* should not stop there as the climax is 4 bars later. By all means drop down a little in bar 39, but perhaps to *mezzopiano* rather than *piano*.

There are several decisions to make regarding touch and treatment of semiquavers. You will see that the LH is *legato* in the opening accompaniment figure and this should continue throughout. In the RH, however, the semiquavers could be played either articulated or smoothly. Certainly, *legato* would be easier, but you must ask yourself why some of the passagework has long slurs, which may suggest a more *staccato* touch for the shorter groups.

A true Allegro should feel like 2 beats in the bar and not 4, but do not begin with too optimistic a tempo. When this piece was set before, examiners heard a fluctuating pulse as early as bar 9 and this varied thereafter depending upon the technical demands. Also, we heard an *accelerando* in the quavers between bars 34 and 42, and the final line caused retarding in the quaver co-ordination with the semiquavers — so look out for the same problems recurring.

Technically, the LH may experience tension in the semiquavers, so use a slight rotary movement to help. Bars 21 and 25 may well have co-ordination problems, and it may help initially to play the LH in chords. The placing of notes where the hand is stretched will always be awkward, and this will occur in bars 28, 30, 32 and 34–41. A slight lateral movement should be used, just as one would use when playing a broken-chord figure.

The fingering, correct though it is, may be confusing in the repeated notes in the RH in the 1st bar and later, and if this is the case, simply use 4 on all the Fs. And for those who are muddled by the changing finger pattern in bars 16 and 58, use 5–4–5 if these fingers are sufficiently strong.

A:3 Alwyn *All Forlorn*

The four pieces which comprise the third choice are all attractive, and there are many technical and musical teaching principles to be found throughout. I think that the Foxtrot (B:3) may be the most popular choice because of the rhythm, but both the slow waltz and this piece will appeal to pupils who like a melody to play. The study (the first alternative) will, of course, be fun for those who can get around the keyboard quickly and who have nimble fingers.

In this Alwyn piece the LH will require quite a large stretch, as the bass note must be held on, and it will be your decision as to which fingering is easiest or possible. The 3rd finger in the 2nd bar should be altered to 2, and in the following bars 1–2–1–2 might be used instead of what is suggested. It can be suggested that the RH could play both top and middle lines in bars 3 and 4, but I am rather unhappy about this, as I like the RH to concentrate entirely on making a good sound.

The piece falls into three sections: the first of 6 bars, then two of 8 bars each. Although there are slurs, each section should sound like one phrase, and one needs to make a focal point in each. This will be the 4th bar in the first phrase, then the *start* of the next section (bar 7), with a long *decrescendo* down to the *rallentando*, and again in bar 18 in the last section. Remember to support all that you do in the RH with the LH.

I expect that we will hear this played too quickly, as the basic notes are fairly simple, and only the most musical candidates like a slow piece to play. So insist on the metronome mark as it will give the right character, which should be sad and wistful.

Finally, remember to lean over towards the upper part of the keyboard *before* the 7th bar, as this should prevent a gap in finding the new position.

B:1 Martin Peerson *The Fall of the Leafe*

The octave chords in the LH will govern the choice of this or A:1, but it would be stylistically permissible to spread them quickly, with the top note played with the RH chord. However, although this method may be easier than hitting the whole chord at once, the bottom D should really be held.

The piece is very formal and serious, so there must be no suggestion of hurrying. Before starting, think of the tempo you will require in the section with semiquavers.

19

The crotchets must be held full-length throughout, even where the LH thumb needs to move (for example in bars 5–6). In bar 7, the RH top D must go smoothly into the C#. If the fingering is difficult in bar 8, then I suggest that the lower part is better broken with another thumb, rather than the top line.

The ornaments are not complicated and should all be played with the beat. Counting may be advisable in bar 12 to place the 4th beat correctly, and this in turn will help to keep the quavers steady in the following bar.

The second half of the piece suggests a chorale and should be played as smoothly as possible: the LH is important here and needs to support the RH with a careful balance. The dynamics overall should have strong contrast, as they will give poise and character to the piece.

B:2 Gurlitt *A Little Flower*

This delicate little piece, with its deceptively simple melody, has the lilt of a waltz, and I think that it would be a good idea to feel that as you play it. The tempo indication should be followed if possible, as one really wants a feeling of 1 in the bar and not 3 equal beats.

It will be important to think ahead, particularly in the short middle section, where nimble and agile fingers will be needed. The technical problems in the quavers will be caused by awkwardly changing hand positions, especially with the thumb having to move forward to the black note in bar 21, and then pull back in bar 22. There is no easier fingering which will produce a smooth effect, so I think that this passage needs to be memorised so that one can look at the keyboard. Fortunately, the LH is not moving. Incidentally, remember to move upwards with the arm, otherwise the fingers will not be over the notes sufficiently quickly.

The first section has two phrases: up to the 8th bar and from there to the 16th. In each phrase, make a small *crescendo* to the 2nd bar and also to the 4th; then fall away in the next 4 bars. The peak of interest overall should be the 23rd bar, and the ending should be very quiet.

Finally, remember to hold the dotted minims in bar 15 and in the penultimate bar.

B:3 Seiber *Foxtrot II*

This needs a good sense of rhythm at quite a fast tempo. Hands need to be independent, as the LH has *staccato* accompaniment throughout, while the RH is melodic.

Examiners will want to hear bright and confident playing which has little need for subtlety of dynamics. Remember that there should be 2 beats in the bar, not 4, and this will help to suggest the restless, jerky style.

It has three clearly defined sections, and I would make the repeat of the theme in bar 25 the loudest, with a good *crescendo* in the preceding 3 bars. Personally, I would play the middle section a little more quietly, as it begins in a minor key. However, there are no dynamics indicated, so you can choose your own.

Be careful with the rhythm in bars 7 and 8, where the steady crotchet beat stops, and also where there are tied notes.

First Alternative T. Lack *Allegro assai in B flat*

Although this is romantic and flowing, it is really a study for moving around the keyboard evenly and steadily with hand interplay. Like all technical pieces, it requires good control of the fingers and reliably changing hand positions before the musical aspect can be considered. Unfortunately, far too frequently, we hear candidates who show flashes of real musicianship in easier sections of a piece, but who fall down because either notes in passagework or finding chords have not been mastered securely.

First of all, isolate the LH and practise in chords, thinking of the width of the hand stretch. For instance, a 5th in bar 1, and a 6th in bar 2. You will find that no interval stretch is more than a 6th even though the notes look like a 7th in the 5th bar. The most awkward places are those where the thumb has a black note to find. The RH has no real problems, but, if you can, bring out the melody line, which falls on the first note of all RH groups. As the whole piece moves up or down approximately an octave in each bar, it would be wise if it could be memorised so that the LH movement could be watched.

The piece has two identical 8-bar sections, so there are only 10 bars to learn. I would suggest that the first *crescendo* goes up to *mezzoforte*, leaving the stronger dynamic for the repeat. Remember that a good *crescendo* means increasing volume on every note, not just accents on the first of each group.

Since this music is based entirely on harmonies, the pedal needs to be changed each half-bar. Ideally, it would sound better if the 2nd and 4th beats could be cleared, as otherwise there may be blurring, especially if the tempo is rather slow. That would mean down on the 1st beat, up on the 2nd, down on the 3rd and up on the 4th.

Second Alternative Gedike *Slow Waltz*

The LH will have to hold quite large intervals here, but fortunately the pedal can help. If it is used, and it ought to be, then it should go down on the 1st beat and be lifted on the 3rd, as *legato* use of pedal is not needed in a waltz.

It is written in three sections, bars 1–16, 17–28 and 29 to the end. Try to give the impression of two 8-bar phrases in the first and third sections, and of one 12-bar phrase in the middle section.

If you follow the suggested dynamics they will help, but it is important to make a focal point in each phrase — for instance, where the cadence falls, in bars 7 and 8 and again in 15 and 16. In the middle section, the *mezzoforte* should be the strongest point, but the *ritardando* will create its own importance.

Grade 4

A:1 L. Mozart *Allegro in G*

This has a strongly defined style which requires poise and elegance and good phrasing, so if the pupil is rather clumsy, and finds even and steady finger control difficult, I would suggest the much more direct style of B:1 by Handel.

I often talk about feeling 1 beat in a bar, but here there should be three distinct quavers with a slight emphasis on the first. The LH notes need separation, like bowing strokes, but hold all longer notes for their full length.

The suggested dynamics should be followed, and also you may wish to rise and fall with the pitch to give shape to individual phrases. For instance, rise to the 3rd bar, go down in the 4th, and let the overall peak of this first section be at the double bar. There can be another *crescendo* going towards bar 34, but the strongest climax must be at the end. If you prefer the immediate contrast of the given dynamics, then no gradual rise and fall with the pitch will be needed. Whatever you choose, however, be consistent.

In the RH repeated chords (e.g. bars 11–12) remember that they must go somewhere, and this will require the LH to provide a *crescendo* for them to follow, as it is the bass line which gives interest here, not the chords.

Technically, most of the movement lies within a hand position or has scalic passages. Co-ordination will need care in bars 10, 22, 30 and 36, and the demisemiquavers must not sound rushed. Certainly, the LH will have to be looked at in bar 10 to find the top D, but fortunately the RH stays on the same notes as in the previous bar. The grace-notes should be played *before* the beat in this piece, as otherwise they would disturb the basic pulse.

A:2 Beethoven *Bagatelle in F*

I think that the popularity of this piece lies in the happy and light-hearted melody and the swinging accompaniment figure. It is usually played quite well, unless hand co-ordination is poor or the hand-span itself is limited. If so, the octave intervals can be helped by using a lateral swing with the wrist.

Grace-notes may prove to be a problem, as they must be put in very quickly before the beat; it may be wise to play them initially together with the main note to *feel* the interval in time. The *sforzando* notes should be emphasised. Within the *piano* sections, they should merely be slightly defined and must not be heavy; within the *forte* sections they can be stronger.

The two main climaxes are fairly obvious — bars 28–30 and the ending, which uses a keyboard range of five octaves. The range of dynamics can be very wide and vivid, and if you want, use *una corda* in the *pianissimo* sections.

At first sight, the phrases look as though they are in 4-bar lengths, but movement is really carried forward, with phrases dovetailing together. For example, the phrase at bar 5 goes on (via the 2nd-time bar) into the next section and does not really stop until bar 16; the repeat of this section drives forward with the LH movement in bar 16*b*, and the RH chords lead the listener on.

Technically, the hand may become tense with the repeated notes, and bars 56–9 will be difficult with the frequent changes of hand position. You will have to look at the keyboard here for safety. Certainly, the changes of fingers will ensure good repetition, as 4 and 5, if used on the top notes, are often too weak. It is with this in mind that the changes of fingers are suggested in bar 29.

It will be your decision as to how to finger the first two bars in the LH. I use 4 for the A, but I understand the editor's suggestion that 3 initially would be stronger. I do, however, find the fingering for the third line rather fussy. I would rather use 5/4 at the start of bar 9, then move the hand to 5/3 in bar 10, then move it down to 5/4 again in bar 11 and up to 5/3 in bar 12. You will find that the 4th finger remains as a common denominator on G.

I must mention pedalling. At the beginning, use *legato* pedal movement for each half-bar for the pattern in the first 2 bars. You could continue this in the next 2 bars, but there may be unwanted blurring, and the rest must have clearance. Use it again to make the chords smooth in bars 16*b* and 17, and I would just touch it briefly to warm the two-note slurs in bars such as 20 and 21 and again later. In the last line, use it for the first two quavers of each three-note pattern, but keep the rests clear in the penultimate bar.

A:3 Heinz Benker *Ballabile*

The four pieces which comprise the third choice are very different in character and in their technical demands. This little waltz has perhaps the most obvious style, with B:3 needing imagination to tell its story, and the two alternatives having mainly technical matters to overcome.

First of all, play the whole-tone scale on which this piece is based, as it will help to 'hear' the tonality. Starting on C, the fingering is 1–2–1–4–3–2 in the LH and 1–2–1–2–3–4 in the RH. In the piece the scalic passages may well have different fingering, but that is only because of the succeeding notes. By far the most awkward of these passages will be in bar 27, but 5–1 is necessary in the RH if a *legato* slur is to be produced. The added difficulty here is the rising LH scale, and this might well be memorised.

The composer suggests that the player may use any dynamics, so you must use your own ideas here. As usual I would crescendo where the pitch rises — for instance, from bar 5 up to 8, and down for the start of 9. Then up again from bar 13 to 17 where I would use *forte*, and this should go on through to the peak of the piece in bar 27. I would drop back to *piano* almost immediately, and rise only slightly in the second last line before ending *pianissimo*.

The pedal can be used to help hold the bass notes on the second page, and I would use it anyway from the beginning, putting it down on the 1st beat and lifting it up on the 2nd.

The dotted minim beat will give the lilt of a waltz, so try to reach the suggested tempo. As the piece is in a free form, bring out the first motif whenever it appears, for example in the LH in bars 21 and 22.

B:1 Handel *Courante in F*

This is straightforward to play, and does not require especial subtlety in tone or touch. It does, however, need crisp *staccato*, articulate and controlled scale passages and a strict pulse.

When it was set before we heard many candidates who began in bar 1 with one tempo and immediately became faster in the next 2 easier bars, only to retard when the semiquavers occurred. There were gaps at the end of bars 9, 10, 11 and 12 as candidates found the LH chords. I also remember that the semiquavers were often rushed, and this usually followed a quaver which was cut short, or occurred after the crotchets in bars 10 and 12. All these faults meant that good marks could not be given. Be careful to look ahead to avoid these mistakes. Another mistake is to look down at the keyboard to find the chord, and then pause in order to find one's place in the music again.

The whole piece is very strong, but follow the suggested dynamics so that the *crescendo* which begins in bar 19 goes through to a *fortissimo* ending. The dotted minim chords in the LH should each become stronger up to bar 14, as the RH does not always have the 1st beat.

The fingering is mainly simple: the hand position will require care from bars 21–3, and I think that it is easier to use 1/3, then 2 and 2 in the LH in bars 19 and 20.

Finally, I think that there could be a *ritardando* in the penultimate bar.

B:2 J.F.F. Burgmüller *Barcarolle*

This composer wrote many very attractive pieces for piano. Many of these are studies which focus on some technical problem, but they are so pleasant to play that studying them is enjoyable.

A barcarolle is a gentle Venetian piece with a slow rhythmic swing, and here the melody has to be very *cantabile* and very controlled so that the weight can be varied to create ever-changing dynamic interest.

It is important to keep the repeated LH chords very quiet, and to change the weight sufficiently to help the RH melody. Balance between the hands is all important, and even if List B is not used for examination purposes, this skill is worth acquiring by learning this piece anyway. Remember too, that when the melody has long notes the tone will die away, and the accompaniment must die away as well.

The structure is very simple, with an introduction and a very short coda framing the melody beginning in bar 13, the middle section of which begins at bar 21. Phrases should not be broken up into 4-bar lengths, so sensitive dynamics will have to be used. The range is limited due to the gentle character of the piece, so use *pianissimo* up to *mezzoforte*, which will occur at the main peak at bar 27. The *sforzando* notes should merely be small accents, and as they are within a *diminuendo* they should have no hardness. This applies to bars 4 and 8 as well, but I think that the 2nd pause bar could be stronger to emphasise the harmony change.

If you are uncertain how to play the melody, then sing it, and this will give you a better idea of how to make it breathe. If you were a string player, the bow would not be *lifted* off between the slurs, but would merely change from a down- to an up-stroke.

The pedal can be used, as this is a lyrical piece, and you may feel that detached chords are too dry: this would mean changing on each half-bar apart from clearance at phrase ends or when harmonies change — for instance, in bar 19. However, the rests in bars 27, 28 and 29 must be kept clear, and if melody notes blur, then the pedal must be lifted or not used at all.

B:3 Kullak *Grandmama tells a ghost story*

I mentioned previously that this would require imagination, and I am sure that a good story can be made up to inspire the colour, texture and touch needed to bring this piece to life. It has several different moods, and should be fun to play.

There *are* some awkward chords to find, and the 3rds will need neat finger agility, but the tempo is not too fast. My advice about looking ahead must be taken seriously here, as in every half-bar there will be something to prepare for: either a hand position change, a thumb on a black note, or an interval leap. So think of what preparation is required when initially learning the notes, as it will be too late when the tempo becomes faster and you have musical qualities to add.

Some fingering may require revision for different sizes of hand. Some suggestions look over-fussy, although they may be correct and logical. For instance, I think that in bar 10, it is easier to keep 5/2 on the first two chords, and then put 4 and 1 on the F# and D. Another query may be the changing fingers in both hands in bar 17, as this might result in inaccurate note-placings.

Try to make *staccato* notes as crisp as possible — imagine going on tip-toe through a big, dark, deserted house, with only a torch for company.

The structure of the first phrase should go up to a peak in the 4th bar and down again to the double bar. Then use the first notes of each short entry in both hands to build up to a really strong *forte* in bar 12, which will die down to the pause. The new *legato* tune at bar 31 is fairly dramatic so the dynamics which follow need to be exaggerated, especially when the LH takes over the melody at bar 40. In bars 36–7 and 44–5 I would suggest emphasising the top E, which should be followed by a strong accent on the LH A.

Remember to hold all the pauses for an extra beat, especially in the empty bar, as there has been a *rallentando* as well.

First Alternative Skütte *Prelude in A minor*

Before the attractiveness of this piece can be appreciated, steady, flowing and fluent technical facility will be needed.

There is a top line to hold smoothly, and although many people may wish to take some of the accompanying notes in the RH, I feel this would interfere with the structure of the phrases. My advice would be to work out which fingering will be needed in the LH thumb turn, and I suggest 4–2 in the 1st bar and 3–2 in the 2nd.

Two similar sections follow which make up the middle section, and they should have the same treatment except for the *mezzoforte* in bar 21, which I feel is the strongest peak in the whole piece. The ending should be as *pianissimo* as possible. *Stringendo* is written and this is very important. It means 'go forward in tempo', and this feeling of moving on is essential to all romantic music. In the middle section, therefore, the speed will have to be faster than the original tempo to offset the gradual slowing down in the last line. It is also useful in creating excitement which will underline the climax bars.

To make sure of hitting the chord-notes together in the 3rd bar and later, practise trying to play the thumb-note before the others. This will offset the physical tendency to play the top note earlier as it lies closest to the previous note.

Overall, try to create a smooth and even semiquaver line which flows up from the LH to the RH. The pedal should be put down on the 1st beat of each bar, with the rests cleared. This piece is very useful to learn apart from using it for examination purposes, as it encourages listening for a good balance and skilful use of *rubato*.

Second Alternative Sartorio *Study in D minor*

With its energetic bass line melody, this piece will encourage strong and independent LH fingers, especially as the semiquaver passages have to be played with different dynamics. Also, the keyboard range is used quite widely, and the LH must move up and down over a span of three octaves. For this, the body must be flexible, to assist the arm and hand in bars such as 4 and 12.

Quite a lot of the melody has different hand positions, which have to be found quickly, and the RH has chords as well, so various parts of the piece may need to be memorised. As I have said before, beware of the common fault of looking at hands, then losing the place in the copy.

The dynamics can be very strong and vivid in the section beginning at the double bar, but keep in mind that the ending should be strongest of all.

The phrases are all 8 bars in length, except the section beginning at bar 17, which is 16 bars long.

Grade 5

A:1 J.S. Bach *Invention in D minor*

The tempo suggestion will let the music flow forward without the quavers becoming slow and laboured, but I think it may be too fast to fit in the trills as written out. Therefore, as these long trills *must* be played and somehow become integrated into the music, I can only suggest a rhythmically free trill, which would be preferable to playing the piece very much slower and losing marks with the loss of the musical character. The trills should be stopped as indicated, so that the tied note can be effective, and very slow practice may be needed here.

The piece falls into three sections, marked by the cadences in bars 17–18 and 37–8. Dynamics within these should not be violent, and in addition to those suggested by the editor, let the rise and fall in pitch be your guide. Also, the 2-bar motif or subject which moves from hand to hand should be brought out wherever it appears. However, in a sequential passage like the second line in the RH and the third line in the LH, you could perhaps make a long *diminuendo* to the cadence. This means that the climax of the first section would be in bar 6, so rise up from the beginning.

I suggest the next section should go through to *its* highest point in bars 36 and 37, and the original entry which returns in both hands from bar 44 can lead either to a strong or quiet ending, depending on your wish. Personally, I feel that it makes a better ending if played decisively.

Technically, it will be helpful to prepare the hand for stretching the 7th interval in the subject — but remember that this is sometimes a *diminished* 7th and that is really a 6th, so the span will have to change. The LH will require care in placing octave leaps, for instance in bars 17, 37 and 38.

A:2 Clementi *Sonata in D, second movement*

Both A:2 and B:2 are expressive movements, and by this grade we expect to hear a really controlled and textured *cantabile* tone quality in a slow movement such as this. If your pupil is 'down-to-earth' and not especially aware of the difference between a superficially thin tone and thick texture, then this piece will be useful for teaching how to put arm weight down into the fingers through a supported but not stiff wrist. This is a lovely piece, but as examiners will only give high marks if they hear beautifully shaped phrasing and a very sensitive range of touch, keep this in mind when choosing the best list for individual pupils.

Let us look at the structure of phrases. Try to think up to the 14th bar with only a small break in the 4th. Good dynamics should take the listener up to the top D as the peak of this section, and although there are *rinforzando* notes, they are within a *piano* dynamic so need only slight emphasis. The *sforzando* in bar 12 is only a *little* louder.

The next section should go through to bar 36, because the repeated pedal As will keep the musical movement flowing from bar 24, just as the Gs kept us moving in bar 8. Of this section, the main focus should be in bars 29 and 30, re-inforced in the next line. This should fall gently into the upward scale passage, rather like a question mark, especially as it ends with a dominant 7th to be resolved.

In the final page, I would take a breath after the *poco ritardando* — the last repeat of the melody deserves a new phrase in itself.

The treatment of the repeated notes should be mentioned. When repetition occurs in bars 8 and 10, it takes us through a *crescendo* to a focal note — in this case, the *rinforzando*. But when the repeated notes form the pedal bass of a harmony, as from bar 24, they must rise and fall with what is happening above, as they are merely an accompaniment.

Pedal can be used in this movement to give warmth and resonance. Rests must be cleared, however, and all harmonies changed cleanly. Only by listening carefully will the pupil do this successfully, and one hears frequent blurring in examinations where the foot is used automatically and the piano action may be different. Not only must one listen to harmonies changing, but one must be aware of the effect of passing notes in various registers of the keyboard.

A:3 Gerard Hengeveld *Cha-cha-cha*

Of the four pieces comprising the third choice, I think it is safe to say that many candidates will choose to play this one, as it is rhythmic and fun to play. The Scherzo (B:3) has the same light-hearted characteristics but is different in tonality, and the predictability of this little dance may be more instantly appealing. The two alternatives involve more complicated technical skills.

Bars where the dotted crotchets occur may invite rhythmic unsteadiness, and these notes should be placed with care. I can foresee that in bars 2 and 18 the last 2 beats will eventually sound like two quavers. Also, there might be an inclination to hurry the three-quaver group, and this must be avoided as the poise of the dance depends on strict rhythmic control. (These problems occurred frequently when the piece was last set in the syllabus.)

Make dynamics as vivid as possible, especially the *piano* in the second line and the accents in bars 13 and 14.

B:1 Scarlatti *Sonata in A*

One can use words such as poise, elegance, charm and gracefulness to describe this piece, and I think that the tempo indication will give just the right effect.

A:1 had the awkward trill problem and, here too, ornamentation features frequently. The actual notes of the ornaments are not difficult or complicated but I feel that many candidates will play them as a triplet of quavers, just as in the 1st bar, but this is not what is intended. So it will be essential to practise very slowly, making certain that the last note of each ornament is placed correctly. Sometimes — as in the 2nd bar — you will have to count in duplets, and sometimes — as in bar 7 — in triplets.

Any commas which occur within a phrase should have only the smallest breath, but those which occur at the end of a section (bars 10, 18, 26, 40, 52 and 60) can have a definite break.

Try to structure phrases with one focus in each: for instance, bring up dynamics in the 5th bar and come down towards the end of the next line. Or use echoes as a means of sustaining interest: for example bars 13–14 might echo 11–12. Certainly, I feel that there should be a good *crescendo* from bar 19 to 26, though once again a small echo may be made in bar 24. This pattern may be followed in the second half, but it will be your decision whether to end strongly or quietly.

Finally, remember that all crotchets which have no slurs should be detached, and played like bowed strokes.

B:2 S. Storace *Sonata in F, first movement*

This is expressive and needs a good *cantabile* tone, but it is more straightforward than A:2 which had the added complication of balance.

There are repeated notes here as well (bar 1) but, as they are part of the melodic line, they must lead the listener's ear to the next main note at the start of the next bar. A gradual *crescendo* should be made in *both* hands, and this can die back in the 4th bar. As there is more movement to the cadence in bar 8, the *crescendo* could be stronger this second time.

The *mezzoforte* in bar 8 can be quite dramatic as the music is very different here, and the semiquavers should be played semi-*staccato*, just as they should later in the piece (bars 43–4). Otherwise, treat all semiquavers smoothly, though for pupils with small hands this will be difficult with the use of the 4th and 5th fingers in bars 20 and 49. Unfortunately, the indicated tempo cannot really be taken any slower, as the crotchets would become too heavy and difficult to handle musically.

You will find that phrases never stop because some quavers carry us into the next new beginning, and this effect must be suggested either by dynamics or onward movement. This applies to the second half of bar 4 and 14 in the first section, and in bar 38 in the second.

A good sense of pulse will be needed, as there are various pitfalls where the rhythm could fluctuate. Whenever semiquavers occur there might be retarding, and when there are triplets following semiquavers I can imagine that they will be too fast and the following duplets will lose the original pulse. Bars 12–14 and 24–6 are good examples. Another possible danger may be to play the quaver in the LH in bars 21 and 22 as a semiquaver, and the RH triplet pattern in bars 24 and 25 as a quaver and two semiquavers.

Keep in mind that the LH should be *legato* throughout except where indicated, and that the accompaniment should always support the melody.

B:3 Henk Badings *Scherzo pastorale*

A:3, the Cha-cha-cha, may have a more direct appeal, but for pupils who like a piece which has humour and is highly individual in character, this will be attractive.

It needs neat and nimble fingers, as the hands are often close together and could easily collide, and also facility in moving up and down the keyboard. It would be a good piece for Aural Test D at this level, as there are many ingredients to identify, so try it out on your pupils when you first play it to them. For instance: did the tempo change? Was it *staccato* throughout? Was there a melody anywhere? Did it remain quiet?

There are three sections: 14 bars of nervous energy, then a more expressive section, and then a recapitulation of 14 bars, which is extended at the end by the long B. The piece is in the key of B♭, and although this is difficult to trace apart from the beginning, you will find that it is resolved finally in the last bar.

It is important to feel 1 beat in the bar, so if the tempo becomes too slow and there seems to be 3 beats, the mark will not be high as the character will lack the agitation required.

Some fingering may be difficult and should be altered to suit the individual hand size and its flexibility. For instance, in the 1st bar, I would use 2–3 in the LH followed by 4–1 in the 3rd bar, and would repeat this pattern before moving the hand up for the next chord. The indicated fingering, however, would prepare the fingers for the chord in bar 7, so you must decide which is safer. These chords could all be played with 2/4 as they are the same interval, and I think that the thumb would be difficult to place quickly in the 8th bar.

In the middle section, some rhythmic problems may arise in bars 16 and 17, and also whenever there is a tied note and no first beat (bars 20 and 23 will be especially awkward).

The dynamics should reach a peak towards the *forte*, and in the second page I would suggest another *crescendo* from the *più mosso* up to bar 38 and through to the accented B. Then, a *diminuendo* to a *pianissimo* ending.

First Alternative
J.F.F. Burgmüller *L'Hirondelle (The Swallow)*

I mentioned earlier that some technical skills would have to be learned from the alternatives. While studies in themselves can be boring and dull for pupils to learn, many of these romantic pieces have good melodies and appealing harmonies. This little study is an excellent example, which benefits further from painting an imaginative picture. You could stimulate pupils' imaginations by describing how swallows dart about very swiftly and then glide in the air — which perhaps explains the *legato* slurs! Even better, show them pictures of the birds themselves.

The technical skill involves crossing hands, and this is something which needs to be taken seriously as one finds awkwardness and clumsiness when it occurs fleetingly in a piece. Candidates who are unused to the physical movement involved will find this piece very helpful.

Initially, prepare pupils by holding a chord with the RH around middle C — the simple triad if you like — and practise swinging the LH from the lower C octave to the C above the RH. When this is comfortable, increase the swing by moving up to the C an octave higher, or starting from the C two octaves below the RH, which should stay in the same place. Then swing to any notes of the triad. This exercise will provide the left-arm motion which will be required. Then practise the piece with the RH playing chords to find the notes initially, before breaking them up as written. I think that this piece must be memorised, as all pianists would have to look at the keyboard for safety.

The piece itself is in two sections, with the first 8 bars repeated, then 14 bars of slightly different material, initially in B minor and including a coda from bar 22 to the end. The composer's dynamics will help to shape each section. The melody lies in the top line and soon becomes lyrical in the slurs which are played by the LH.

To gain high marks in this piece, we would expect even and very steady interplay between the hands, a defined melody and contrast in the lyrical slurs. A common fault will be in the RH, which will run the semiquavers together, with a resulting gap in continuity.

Pedalling can be used but, together with the other technical difficulties, it may be too much to think about. If it is used, then use it very quickly on the bass notes and lift immediately, but use *legato* pedalling in the slurred melodies, changing on each crotchet. Obviously, if the first pattern is too complicated, then confine pedalling to the longer sustained slurs.

Second Alternative
Haberbier *Prelude in E minor*

As the footnote says, this piece is an excellent study for interweaving notes between the hands and, like the hand-crossing skills in the Burgmüller piece, this technique needs practice.

Apart from the more obvious requirement not to collide, the musical aspect involves smooth and even control, so that the listener has no clue as to *what* has been played with which hand. In this example, any takeovers are in the middle line of writing, and of course, it is important that there are no accents in the middle of a slur (for instance in the 2nd and 4th bars, with the RH thumb). It will be helpful if the middle voice is practised alone. (This skill will eventually be used in preparing a more complicated fugue in later grades.) You will find that a few bars have four-part writing: they are 6, 7, 14–16 and the ending, but there is no overlapping involved.

I think that this Prelude is awkward to play, and pupils may find the close proximity of the hands uncomfortable. The top line melody has to be sustained as well, and there is much stretching in both hands, including frequent use of thumbs on black notes.

There are two 8-bar phrases, but then the next phrase must go from the half-bar of bar 16 to the end. Fortunately, the long *crescendo* which begins at bar 20 up to the *forte* will help to keep the interest before the long descent in pitch, and its accompanying *diminuendo*, to the finish.

Grade 6

GROUP A

A:1 B. Marcello *Sonata in G, second movement*

The choice of A:1 or A:2 will depend upon whether the pupil concerned has quick, even and light-fingered agility in both hands, or whether fairly predictable scalic passagework in the LH would be easier for examination purposes. The actual passagework is more demanding in this sonata movement, and the hands could become tense and stiff unless rotary movement is naturally available.

It is interesting to note that the melody of the first line is not used again throughout the movement, although the material in the second line is repeated frequently. Because there is so much repetition you will find that a number of echoes have been suggested, but apart from this remember the rule of dynamics rising and falling with the pitch of the music. For instance, go up to the 2nd bar and come down in the 4th.

In the second line, the RH notes which are parallel to the LH should be brought out, and this rule should be followed throughout. A decision will have to be made regarding touch, and both semi-*staccato* and *legato* would be acceptable. In the second line, you may wish to use in the RH the slurs and articulation suggested in the LH, thereafter varying the touch in bars such as 9 and 10. Whatever you decide, remember to make it consistent.

In the second half of the piece, use the repeated notes to crescendo into the next bar, but the *mezzoforte* should be slightly quieter in the next 2 bars before beginning quite a strong build-up to bars 27 and 28. Remember that crotchets and *staccato* quavers in the LH should be played lightly, like string bowing strokes.

The RH passagework should not prove to be too difficult as it lies comfortably within a hand position, but the LH may have problems with the varying intervals in the second half, so it may help to practise initially in chords before playing as written.

A:2 Bertini *Study in C minor*

Firstly, it would be a good idea to practise the LH alone until the thumb turns become effortless and comfortable. The arm is going to need lateral movement to lead the hand up and down over a range of three octaves. The RH has a completely different role to play, and this too should be isolated, to learn the many necessary changes of fingering required to sustain the top line, and also to hold the lower part. Try if possible to bring out the upper part of the RH, and once you begin to consider the piece musically, think horizontally not vertically.

In the first section make a small *crescendo* towards the 4th bar, and again towards the 8th. The peak should be the 13th bar, with an echo in the next sequence, but the *forte* in bar 17 will have to be strong to create a convincing *diminuendo* to bar 22. The ending itself could be either *forte* or *piano*, but if you choose a strong ending then crescendo up to it in bar 25.

Remember to lean downwards with your body in the penultimate line and up again for the 24th bar — if possible, *before* it is required. This piece will rely on thinking ahead quite quickly, as the tempo indication is a good Allegro, and the overall effect should be 2 beats in the bar.

Ideally, this piece should be memorised, as it would be much easier to play when looking at the keyboard, especially in finding the octave intervals in the LH.

GROUP B

There are two very attractive choices in this group, and both are very different in character. The Clementi is beautifully expressive and will need a really textured *cantabile* with an awareness of balance under the melody. The Mozart was a popular choice when we set it before in the syllabus, as it is light-hearted and requires no great depth of understanding apart from expressing elegance and poise.

B:1 Clementi *Sonata in F sharp minor, second movement*

One of the problems of this piece will be to keep it moving forward at a very slow tempo. It could so easily become static and dull, with accented quavers, and this would mean that it would be boring and without shape. Although the first phrase would seem to stop in the 4th bar, try to think of the first 13 bars as one section, and move on slightly in the second line to take the listener through to the *sforzando*.

In the first phrase of the next section, it would be a good idea to crescendo slightly up to bar 16 and come down in the following bar. This phrase does not stop in bar 17 because of the moving semiquavers, and pushes on. Dynamics can be really dramatic here, but although the double *forte* in bar 20 is very strong, the real climax will come after emphasis on all the notes in bar 24. In bars 23 and 24 the touch must carry a lot of weight in order to make a graduated *crescendo*, which should continue to the end of the trill. Remember that the LH should support all RH dynamics.

Then the recapitulation begins, mixing material heard in the previous two sections. This time the music does not break *at all* until the end, and so must be structured similarly.

Let us go back to the very first line. The semiquavers of bar 1 need to lead us to the emphasised 1st beat in the 2nd bar, and similarly to the 3rd bar with its ornamentation. At no time in this piece should the faster notes sound rushed, and this applies especially to the demisemiquavers, which should be treated as part of the melody.

As this is a slow piece, one of the refinements required is an awareness of how the notes die away. At the beginning, for instance, one must listen to the dying volume of the tied note and echo this *diminuendo* in the two accompanying chords. This occurs throughout this line, and that is why one must keep bringing the semiquavers up in volume to offset an ever-decreasing *diminuendo*.

In bars 21–3, although there will be very slight gaps in the RH to place the notes, the LH must give the impression of a sustained slur, and therefore the pedal should catch the end of each crotchet to join them while the RH moves. Also in this passage, the lower line of the RH should be brought out in the first half-bar, then the top line in the next half-bar; but all within the *piano* dynamic before the *crescendo* begins.

Pedalling is vital to give sonority and resonance, so change it with the LH notes at the beginning, as although the harmony remains the same for the two chords, the quaver should be separated from the crotchet. Obviously, rests must be observed with no pedal, and it should be lifted for the chromatic semiquavers in bar 3.

In the next line, I would suggest holding it through the crotchet, lifting it for the rest and touching it again for the quaver. However, if the piano action seems to blur the semiquavers badly, then do not use pedals here.

This will apply also to the new section beginning at bar 14, where the demisemiquavers need to be clear. Remember that all quavers should have separate pedal depression, as the quaver is the beat. This occurs in bars 9, 20, 41–2, 46–8 and the penultimate bar.

B:2 Mozart *Sonata in E flat, second movement*

The first of these minuets delineates its dance rhythm most clearly, and so it is comparatively simple to lighten the 3rd beat and emphasise the 1st. This can be applied as well to the six-quaver bars, where the motion leads us forward to the beginning of the next bar.

The strong chords after the double bar are dramatic and different, and they lend weight and interest to an otherwise light and elegant movement. It is important that the top note comes *with* the beat, as if it comes afterwards the decisive pulse would be diffused. With this rhythmic emphasis in mind, make sure that the dotted rhythms are exact with no suggestion of a lazy semiquaver. This is especially important in the bar of thirds, which may be difficult to play.

Dynamics should be followed, but even within the first 4 bars make the second small phrase slightly stronger as it is higher in pitch. If you do not like this idea, then use the written dynamics as *subito* changes and keep this approach consistent. Personally, in bars 24–6 I like a slight *crescendo* up to the top E♭ and then a *diminuendo* down, as I find the sudden *piano* unconvincing.

Usually, a second similar movement is in the tonic minor key for contrast, but this second minuet achieves variety through faster note values and in giving the 3rd beat of the bar melodic importance, which means that it will lead to the next bar. The *subito* dynamics with accompaniment support as well give some added importance to the 3rd beat.

This movement is basically more lyrical because of the moving quavers in the LH, but despite this the RH should observe all articulation slurs and *staccato* notes. Remember to hold crotchets in the LH as long as possible for harmonic sonority.

In bar 47 be careful to play the 1st beat in strict rhythm: when this piece was set previously in the syllabus, we frequently heard this group played as two semiquavers and a quaver. In the following bars, check the rhythmic pattern and ensure that the semiquaver is correct, as previously this was often played as two quavers. Also watch the triplets in bars 37–9: sometimes these were played as quickly as the semiquavers.

Another slight problem was the basic tempo. Many candidates started Menuetto 1 at the suggested speed but when the second more difficult dance began, the pulse immediately retarded. There can be a little licence here, but it should not be very noticeable, so think of the start of the second dance before beginning to play the whole piece. And when restarting Menuetto 1 at the *Da Capo* do not immediately resume a much faster tempo.

The phrases in Menuetto 2 are 8 bars in length throughout, and this differs from Menuetto 1 where there is a 12-bar phrase, then 6 bars plus 14. I mention these lengths to help you create the structure for your pupils. If you are using *subito* dynamics, you must decide which *forte* is to be strongest to focus the listener on the main peak of any section. For instance, the sudden *legato* quavers in Menuetto 1 should provide the focus for the first 12 bars, but they in turn lead to the *forte* imperfect cadence.

Another good example is in Menuetto 2 after the double bar, where there is a repetition of *piano* and *forte* dynamics. If all played the same, they would make this 8-bar phrase meaningless. However, if you begin very quietly, with only a *mezzopiano* dynamic instead of *forte*, and increase this pattern until the true *forte* is reached in bar 53, plus a heavier and very slightly *slower* semiquaver group in bar 55, then you have created a shapely and meaningful phrase, which is an important one as it leads to the recapitulation.

GROUP C

Before I talk individually about the four pieces in Group C, let us compare them for technical difficulty. There are three very romantic choices, which will require sensitive balance, *cantabile* tone and fluency of pedalling. The fourth piece is Bartók's *Dance with Sticks*, which requires a more straightforward approach and vivid dynamics but is not otherwise difficult to play. The pedalling is not subtle but must be used fairly irregularly.

The easiest of the three lyrical pieces is the Jensen (C:4); a warm singing melody line is essential, but *legato* pedalling can be used fairly automatically.

There is little to choose between the Chopin and the Heller pieces, as the former looks deceptively easy but has many subtleties of touch and balance, and the latter is difficult with an accompanying figure and a melody to control in the RH alone. It would be unwise to play the Etude unless the hand is fairly large and is very flexible.

In all three, *rubato* is *essential* if the character of the music is to be expressed and, as I have emphasised before, this means that the tempo at times has to go faster than the basic pulse, so a good degree of technical fluency will be required.

C:1 Chopin *Cantabile in B flat*

This composer produces many problems for young pianists, as the romanticism is intense and sophisticated, and the results we hear are often contrived. *Rubato* reaches its real refinement in this style of writing, as one has to exaggerate so much but must stop short of vulgarity and sheer sentimentality. The balance of getting faster and slower must be offset with very sensitive awareness of shading and nuance in the melody and accompaniment. A warm, rich tone is essential.

Every semiquaver matters in this piece, either lyrically, or as a means forward to a focal note, or to pull back, which will create a similar emphasis. The first phrase lasts 4 bars, but the LH chords force us to listen onwards as the new phrase begins, so try to think of an 8-bar phrase instead. This sense of unbroken line is emphasised by the rests which occur in the 8th bar but not before.

The next two short phrases are simply a coda: you will find that the piece could easily end if you play the first beat in bar 8 and then add the final 2 bars. In order to make the ending interesting, go up a little in the semiquavers in bar 9 towards the C in bar 10. There will then be some *diminuendo* left for the next 4 bars. If this is not done, the *smorzando* chords may well not sound, and, if you have not used *una corda* earlier, then use it here.

In the first line, I would suggest moving on in the 2nd bar towards the G in the 3rd bar, with a slight rise in volume as well to the top B♭: to do this you must bring up the LH chords in support of the dotted quaver B♭ which will begin to die away. Then, this onward movement must be paid back in the triplets in bar 3, which should be treated lyrically and quite slowly at the end.

Remember that two similar bars should be treated differently, as otherwise they will lack interest. Here bars 8 and 10 are very nearly the same, and you might like to give one a *rallentando* and move the other on.

42

I want to mention pedalling, as pianists may be confused by the *staccato* notes and the need to sustain the harmonies. If playing this piece in concert, one would use a very sensitive and delicate lacework of pedalling which would allow the slightly detached *staccato* note to come through but would also sustain it partially. One cannot even say that it is half-pedalling, although this skill is partly involved. None of us would expect this type of effect in a Grade 6 examination, so I would advise *legato* pedalling, every half-bar, which will give the best overall resonance. However, there should be a slight gap to show the beginnings of new phrases, and in bars like 4, the first half of 6, 8 and 10 the pedal should be changed on each quaver. I would change the pedal on each quaver in bars 12 and 13 as well, as there are rests and no harmony notes to sustain.

C:2 Bartók *Dance with Sticks*

This is a strong and vivid piece which must be presented with conviction to bring it off successfully, so avoid any hint of shyness and timidity. Dynamics are mainly loud, and *sforzando* notes can be fairly hard and percussive. A few gentler phrases are suggested which are lyrical, and they will create a bigger contrast for the following *crescendo*.

The LH is variously accented by sustained *tenuto* lines throughout. There are large leaps between the beats, and the pedal has to be used *exactly* as indicated to get the right effect. Often, it should be depressed again *after* the chord has sounded at bar beginnings, and it is important that the hand still holds the notes until the pedal is depressed.

There are two 8-bar phrases, varied slightly in both hands, and I would make the second phrase-ending the stronger. Then comes a section of 16 bars, and although there is a *piano*, the LH keeps it moving through to bar 32. This is then repeated and, with its *allargando*, the ending becomes the climax of the piece.

It is essential that all details of slurs, lined and *staccato* notes are played, as they will bring the piece to life. Otherwise it would simply sound noisy and unattractive. If possible, try to play all LH slurred chords without accents: some will have fingering which can be played smoothly, as in bars 5 and 6, but others will have to rely on pedalling.

C:3 Heller *Etude in D*

This is a very beautiful study, with a lovely melody and a simple balanced bass, and it is satisfying to play if one likes really romantic and expressive music.

The secret of success will lie in handling the triplet semiquavers, which should murmur quietly throughout, almost unnoticed. They provide the driving power to move on or pull back, and also the dynamics to shape the phrases.

If this piece is played too slowly, it will sound like a dull exercise in holding top notes smoothly, with probably too loud and obtrusive an accompaniment. So first play the melody and the LH alone and, when the shape and structure has become clear, learn the inner notes whilst always keeping in mind the skeleton.

There are technical problems to overcome apart from the RH balance: the octave stretches in the third and fourth lines, for instance, some of which cannot be held by the pedal, as it will be changing (for example in bars 13 and 15).

Pedalling should be used throughout, but where there are rests in the melody line they should be kept clear. For instance, the *legato* movement should be lifted at the end of the 2nd bar and the 4th, so that the rests will indicate the new phrases.

Rubato must be used and the general rule would be to move on to the peak of dynamic interest and slow down at the *diminuendo*. For instance, forward in bars 5 and 6 and back in 7. Certainly, there must be an important *rallentando* in bar 20, to lead into the return of the melody in the next bar; but *ease* into the original tempo gradually, not immediately.

Build from bar 23 to the main climax in bar 29, where the accents can be quite strong on the top line. There is another *forte* later, but this is only within the coda bars and signals a gradual *diminuendo* to the end.

C:4 Jensen *Romanze*

This is essentially sad and wistful with a more dramatic middle section, and requires lyrical and expressive playing, with a good *cantabile* tone, a balanced LH, and carefully used pedal. The long phrase lengths will need sensitive dynamics and balanced *rubato* to keep the music moving forward.

The first phrase *could* stop at the 8th bar, but because of the LH movement I feel that one should stop at bar 16 instead. From this point, agitation enters with condensed quaver movement and changes of key, and this section should not end until bar 56. The dynamics must guide the listener on from bar 29 as the pitch rises, right up to the *forte* in bar 37, and although there are a few quieter chords thereafter, the sudden drama in bars 46–8 must keep us in suspense as to where the music is going. This in fact only resolves with the falling semiquavers in bars 57–8, leading back to the restatement of the opening melody.

There are a few longer notes to hold in both hands, and sometimes the pedal will not be able to help. In bar 47, the 10th can be played with the D♯ as a grace-note, but it is vital that the pedal catches this important note of the harmony.

At no point in the final three lines should there be any sense of hurrying in the faster ornamental groups; they must fall lazily into the melodic line structure. If the semiquavers in bars 57 and 58 are really awkward, then some may be played with the LH — for instance the last G and B in bar 57 — but whatever you choose to do, the listener must hear no accents as the hands take over from each other.

Grade 7

GROUP A

The two pieces in this group are similar in concept and style, yet could not be more contrasted. The Scarlatti Sonata is the more direct and obvious, yet requires skill in retaining a *legato* line for four pages without an obvious break, while the Fugue by Bernard Stevens will need a pianist with much patience, concentration and technical refinement to structure and present it successfully and convincingly.

A:1 Scarlatti *Sonata in B minor*

This piece does not divide into obvious sections with cadence points indicating breaks in continuity, and so the successful performance should lead the listener from start to finish in one long continuous phrase.

One should regard all the articulation slurs as very small breaths — unjoined notes if you like, but certainly not as phrase-length indications. They will help to sustain interest. So too will the suggested dynamics, and one needs to supplement these by using the rise and fall in pitch almost imperceptibly to rise and fall in volume. This will give a fluidity and a feeling of onward movement, as at no point should the pulse feel static and laboured.

First of all look for climax points and build towards these bars. Examples are bars 6 and 7, up to the trill in bar 10, and bar 16. In the second half of the piece there should be a slight emphasis to round off bar 27 but the peak of the whole piece must be bar 31, which should be marked not only by a *crescendo* but also with *allargando*. From this focal point fall peacefully and gently to the end.

Remember that in this type of music, *forte* does not mean a hard and strident tone quality, so the range of dynamics is not wide, but requires sensitivity of colour and a real *cantabile* control. Balance of hands is very important, and the bass harmony line must always be kept in mind. For instance, look at bars 4–6, 11–16 and 22–30.

Use echo effects as another way to create interest whenever repetition occurs. For example, you could use it at the end of bar 2, in the second half of bar 7 and in bar 12.

From the 4th bar, use both hands in creating the build-up to bar 6, and remember the rests in the following few bars, as they will give a slight feeling of breathlessness as one moves forward to the trill in bar 10. There is no harmonic resolution here, and the bass C#s keep us in suspense until the double bar. But even here the music does not rest, and bars 18 and 19 lead on to the next section, which has similar pedal-note F#s taking us through to a few extended bars at the end.

Technically, the downward semiquavers in the LH will be difficult to manage smoothly in these sections, and I would suggest practising with the middle finger held down and swinging from the top thumb note down to the lower octave. For instance, in bar 5, the 3rd finger will hold C#, and the thumb will go from G to G. Do not just practise going downwards, as it is important to loosen the wrist laterally in both directions; also, remember to use very little elbow movement. This pattern is more difficult on the second page as there is an added twist from a white middle note to a black key, but once again there must be a smooth thumbjoin, as any break will result in an unwanted accent.

The RH fingering in bar 17 may seem rather unnecessary, but the suggestions for the 5th finger are to keep the hand close to the keys, which should eliminate any accents on the beginning of the slurs. This problem is frequently encountered in examinations, where each small slur has unwanted emphasis and interrupts the direction of the music.

A:2 Bernard Stevens *Fuga alla Sarabanda*

This proved to be one of the most stimulating pieces to study when I came to write this commentary. It is, at first sight, a fugue with various entries of the subject in a Sarabande idiom, but when one begins to dissect it, the skill of the writing becomes increasingly impressive. In all, it is a most rewarding piece to study, but it will take time and a lot of thought and musical skill to play well.

The subject itself deserves thought even before identifying wherever it occurs. It uses all twelve notes of the octave and it is important that it ends on the same note as it begins. For instance, the first entry on E should end on the second note of the 4th bar, and this pattern should be followed for each entry.

The tonality is interesting. The entries do not follow standard rules of classical tonality but take us through various keys. However, E proves to be the tonal centre, as the piece effectively begins in E minor, contains another entry on E in bar 28, and ends, quite beautifully, with an E major chord.

All the entries are *legato* with one small breath in each 3rd bar, and this should be followed carefully. Independence of fingers is important, as pedal-use will not be wise with such clean chromatic contrapuntal writing. The RH frequently plays two parts, each line moving independently, sometimes with a subject to be defined in the upper or lower voice. The LH sometimes has to help with the middle part (for instance, in bars 19, 27, 34 and 39), and the listener must not know that the hands have changed over. To do this successfully, isolate each part and trace its path separately. This will quickly identify the subject in each of the three voices, and immediately some clear structure will become apparent.

It is always very important to think horizontally when working at a fugue: far too often, we hear performances which have obviously been practised from bar to bar, and all sense of the line is lost. It can help to think of three voices — soprano, tenor or alto, and bass. Or, if you know strings better, then think of a violin, viola and cello. Practise top and bottom lines together, then top and middle, then middle and bass — all of this will assist when the *ear* finally takes over from learning the notes and a musical structure is formed.

I mentioned earlier that all the subject entries are *legato*, and that is true of entries which have the original rhythmic pulse. But there are two very important entries which are augmented in length, and these are both entirely detached and defined. They should take precedence over any other presentation of the subject. The first begins in bar 21 on the same note as the previous subject ends, although now in the bass voice, and lasts until bar 27. The next is in the soprano line, and starts in bar 28 and ends in bar 34. This second example is difficult to play well, as the RH has a *legato* inner part to hold.

Shape each entry of the subject with a small *crescendo* and *diminuendo*, so that the next entry can be clearly defined. The general dynamics rise from *piano* at the beginning to *mezzopiano* and *mezzoforte*, and then to *forte* by bar 28 and to *fortissimo* where the pulse begins to be pulled back in bar 32. The piece slows down from bar 39 and falls away to the ending which is *pianissimo*. Use the structure of these dynamics to help shape the piece overall.

GROUP B

The two pieces in this group are similar in idiom and character — both are fast movements from sonatas and both require finger dexterity in passagework. Otherwise, the Haydn demands light and elegant phrasing, while the Beethoven has a more 'down-to-earth' strength.

B:1 Haydn *Sonata in E, first movement*

The tempo indication is lively without being too fast and will let the music breathe without being rushed in the passagework. This is essential to give poise and placing to the phrases. (This is one aspect which goes seriously wrong in many examinations since candidates do not like silences and often cut short rests, and I think examiners write that comment more frequently than any other from Grade 1 upwards.)

The movement has a clearly defined exposition, development and recapitulation. Throughout, the phrase should be thought in long lengths and not every 2 bars, as otherwise the piece will seem very long and broken up.

The first phrase of the exposition is 8-bars long — so think of the first 4 as a question, asked quietly, with a strong 4-bar answer. The following 8 bars are broken up into 4 bars containing a more lyrical idea and 4 of passagework. A further 8 bars complete the first section.

The first 4 bars can be interpreted in two ways, depending on whether you think the 4th bar is more important than the 2nd. If you do, I would start *mezzopiano* and make a slight *diminuendo* in the 2nd bar, and then make a *crescendo* to the 4th. This would lead to the last chords of bar 4, which are *staccato* and accented, and would be better than trying to play all 4 bars *mezzopiano*.

In the second subject (bar 9), make a slight *crescendo* towards the middle of the 2nd bar, but this must not be too strong, as it would diffuse the impact of the sudden *forte*.

Apart from the more lyrical passages, most of the material involves quick and agile fingers, which must be even and steady with no obvious accents or clumsy thumb turns. It is in these pieces where scalic runs occur, that consistent practice of scales and arpeggios will help greatly and where the fingering patterns can be used quickly and without thought. Certainly, I would advise automatic use of scale fingering, as this is easier to remember than those indicated suggestions which do not

49

lie in the usual pattern. For instance, I would start bars 17 and 18 with a 4 in the LH, not 5, as that is the finger pattern for B major. Aim overall for a slightly articulate touch in all passagework.

As one would expect, the development is a mixture of the various ideas we have already heard and has also much harmonic interest which should be defined. This occurs especially in bars 34–40, and so the RH thumb notes should be slightly emphasised in bars 34 and 35 with a supporting balance in the LH, and then the top note brought out in the broken chords in the next 2 bars. In bars 38 and 39, however, the RH moving inner notes are important, followed by the LH moving octaves.

Use the general rule of going up and down slightly with dynamics to follow the rise and fall of pitch in passagework, unless there is a strong reason for doing otherwise. One such instance is the falling scale passage in the 6th bar, which should have a *crescendo* to take us to the trill.

You will find that echo effects are suggested, and these should be followed as they are very effective in this style of writing and add interest to passagework. Examples are bars 13 and 14, 34 and 35, and 54 and 55.

Remember that repeated notes should never sound the same and should go towards a goal — either in a *crescendo*, or dying away. This occurs in bars 29, 30 and 31, and each group of quavers should rise a little louder in each bar, with the final peak rising in bar 32 to the trill. In this way 5 bars which could sound repetitious and unmusical at the same *forte* level can have meaning and forward momentum.

Certain sections of the passagework will cause tension if rotary movement is not used, in particular the broken chords in the development section. I would also use it in passages where the thumb needs to be brought out, as the actual roll towards the bottom note of each group will accent the thumb with no need for further stress. This is in bars 13 and 14, and again later.

I would like finally to mention use of pedal. Frequently we hear dry and brittle Mozart or Haydn, especially in slow movements or lyrical passages, and it should be realised that warmth and resonance can enhance so much music of this period if used imperceptibly. In this movement I would touch the pedal briefly on longer notes; for instance on the crotchets in bars 15 and 16, and on each quaver in bars 29, 30 and 31 (except for the rests, which should remain clear). In bars 36–40, it should be changed with the harmony: remember that the bass will indicate where to change, except in bar 38 where the RH has quaver-length harmonies.

The main problem I shall expect to hear from the examiner's point of view will be a varying tempo, with the candidate starting too optimistically (where it is comparatively easy), and slowing when the semiquavers occur. Bars 17–22 are especially awkward, with good hand interplay and co-ordination required, and I shall also look out for possible retarding with the LH in bars 29–31. Conversely, if too slow a tempo is chosen so that the whole piece can be played with a steady pulse, the effect will be laboured, and it will be very difficult to bring to life with the necessary vitality and sparkle.

B:2 Beethoven *Sonata in E flat, third movement*

The form of this is readily apparent, with the rondo theme occurring four times with three different sections between each statement. What is rather interesting, however, is that these sections vary in length, being 28, 27 and 20 bars each, yet they do not seem unbalanced in performance.

I think for examination purposes that this piece is more difficult than the Haydn. Whereas that fell fairly comfortably under the finger and hand positions, this has broken-chord passagework, and while much of it lies within an octave span, it often involves stretches and leaps, as in bars 24–8. Obviously, practising in chord patterns initially will assist in learning the notes, and in bars such as 13, 14 and 15 I would advise using 1–5 on the octaves if the suggested 4th finger upsets the hand position.

The added complication is the touch, as the movement will sound inarticulate and characterless unless the slurs and *staccato* indications are followed. This in turn will probably dictate a slower initial tempo, with the possibility of the music becoming dull and overlong. I know from experience that candidates usually find it difficult to detach the *staccato* note from the slur before, and I can foresee many instances, for example in bar 9 and later, where the 3-note slur will become a 4-note slur before *staccato* notes are heard. For most candidates, the octave will be the extent of the comfortable hand span and as these notes have to be played *staccato*, the effort to do this may cause a lot of tension. There is little time for rotational help, so the *staccato* notes have to be lifted entirely with the finger-energy.

Co-ordination may also prove difficult, not just where both hands play semiquavers (as in bar 15), but when the RH has quick ornaments to fit in, starting on the beat and coinciding with LH passagework (bars

17–20). Certainly, it would be helpful to practise initially with strong LH accents on the half-bars. I think that the slowest tempo to gain high marks, if everything else is correct and musical, would be the dotted crotchet at 66.

So far, I have talked about possible difficulties. Now let us look at the musical interpretation.

The overall style is quite strong and happy, and should have a swinging pulse of 2 in a bar; regardless of tempo choice this *must* be present if a good mark is to be given.

In the theme itself, go towards the 3rd bar with a slight *crescendo* — but it must be very small, as it is within a *piano* section. Otherwise, the impact of the *subito forte* octaves would be lessened. The dynamic indications and suggestions will help to give interest, but remember that when a sequence of *fortes* and *pianos* occurs it must go somewhere: for example, in bars 17–21 each *forte* should be stronger to lead us through to the peak at bar 23. Do not forget to apply the same principle of dynamics to the LH as well, and apply this rule throughout the movement.

Echoes are variously suggested in repeated passages, and overall the range of dynamics can be very wide, as illustrated in the second episode beginning at bar 45. This section can have a lot of contrasts, as it has minor harmonies as well, especially in the B♭ minor section at bar 63. The pause chord in bar 71 can be strong or quiet, depending upon your choice. Just keep in mind the following repeat of the theme which is *piano*. The last episode also starts in C minor (upbeat to bar 80), and should also be strong and forceful until the lyrical section beginning at bar 88. It is important to hold the notes with the fingers, as although pedal can be used, there must be clarity in the passing-note semiquavers. Much will also depend upon the piano action.

Quite a number of the difficulties in finding notes and larger intervals quickly can be made easier by memorising, and this will certainly be needed in bars 28–33. In the 3rds in bar 33 I use different fingering which I find easier. It is 3/5 on D and F, 2/3 on B♭ and D, 2/4 on the mordent, 1/3 on B♭ and D and 1/2 on A and C. Another section which should be memorised is bars 56–61, and I would suggest you find different fingerings for the first 4 bars. Try to find a pattern that is the same coming down and going up — otherwise, it will be confusing and there will be no logic in the hand positions.

The pedal should be used at various points, starting with the pattern at bar 9, where it should be depressed briefly at each half-bar — no more than a quaver-length. By bar 17, it can be held for the first half of each

bar until bar 22, and do this again on the first half of each bar in 52 and
53. Also, pedal across the slurred semiquavers in 96 and 97.

The most common problem is bound to be a fluctuating tempo which
will retard when the passagework occurs and pick up again when the
theme returns. Also, the treatment of slurs and *staccato* may be very
inconsistent. I think that the mordents will cause hesitation in the RH at
bar 17, and I will listen for possible rushed slurred notes to allow time
to find the next interval at bar 28. At bar 56, I would expect that the
two-note slurs will be hurried with gaps between them, and also
there will be a tendency to run together the 5-finger pattern at bars 45
and 63.

There is much to learn from studying this Rondo, so even if you do
not use it in an examination, it is well worth playing.

GROUP C

Before I talk individually about the four pieces in this group, I would
like to compare them regarding technical difficulty. They are all very
different in character, so one at least should suit your candidate and all
would be useful for addressing various teaching problems.

For only average technical facility, the Cadiz Tango (C:2) would be my
choice, but only if there was a good sense of rhythm and syncopation.

The Toccata (C:1) may be chosen by many candidates, I think, as it can
be effective even if not exactly steady, and what is really required is
agility to get around the keyboard quickly and a violent range of
dynamics.

The Periwinkle (C:3) will suit anyone who can hold the melodic line
and bass, as the pedal will change on every beat. This piece also requires
a large hand-span and a flexible lateral wrist movement in both hands.
Also, a wide but sensitive range of colour is essential, and *rubato* must be
exaggerated if the music is to come to life, as it is very romantic.

Finally, the Heller piece (C:4) is very awkward to play with the spread
chords, which have to be put in before the beat so that the top line is
always steady. Quick pedal movement is essential.

C:1 Edwin Carr *Toccata*

When I indicated above that this piece might not be exactly steady, let
me hasten to say that the exact note values are complex in some bars,

and unless one has a very strong sense of pulse, it will be difficult to play what the composer has written in such detail.

It is essential to use the metronome indication, as if too slow a tempo is used all sense of continuity and structure will be lost. Also, try to think of the most awkward bars before starting, so that the 1st bar — which is easy to play — will not be too optimistic.

You may find it useful to count in quavers in bars 11, 12 and 15. Also, as the composer has written stem-lines to clarify the rhythm in the penultimate bar, one should try to play what is so precisely detailed. Getting around the keyboard quickly is going to be awkward, so be ready to lean towards top and bottom registers when required — if possible, *ahead* of the actual notes. The dynamics are fairly violent and *fortissimo* tone can be strident and hard. The composer has been very precise in indicating the dynamic effects and also the use of the pedal, so we must try to interpret the piece as he would wish.

In bar 9 I play the last two semiquavers with the LH to give time to find the next notes in the RH. In bar 13 I play the first three notes in the RH then three in the LH and the final five with the RH. I use the following fingering for this last group: 5–1–4–3–2.

C:2 David Gow *Cadiz Tango*

I think this will be a popular choice as the rhythm is attractive and one can use one's imagination. I like to think of a throbbing guitar with dancers swirling around in dramatic colours of black and scarlet. This piece relies almost entirely on strong dynamics and a restlessly incessant rhythmic drive.

The original concept of a Tango used a triplet-duplet pattern in a 2-beat bar. Here, although there are many bars constructed with two groups of 3 plus 4 quavers, we also have 3, 4, 5 and 6 quavers in some bars. As most of the piece is in $\frac{7}{8}$, isolate the other bars by marking them, and remember to count carefully in quavers, as exact rhythm is very important.

The dynamics should be followed to give an overall structure which leads to an exciting ending — the strongest part of the piece. Of course the RH should support the LH throughout, except where it takes over the melodic interest in the final three lines.

The short cadenza can be played very freely, at the player's choice. I like to start the long group of quavers slowly and then run into the next accented note, and the *allargando* should be very slow and quite heavy.

At the start of the second page, I think that it heightens the gradual excitement and intensity if one begins slower than the chosen tempo, and so for the first few bars there will be an *accelerando* into the normal pulse. If you want to think in phrases, they begin in bars 7, 20, 26 and 35, but it is better to start the second page *pianissimo* and build up in one long phrase to the *fortissimo* ending. Resist any impulse to make a *rallentando* in the final bar.

The only real difficulty will be in playing the grace-notes very quickly before the accented quaver beats in bars 12, 14 and 32; if the interplay is awkward and clumsy, it may be easier to play all the notes in the RH and to lean on the thumb to make the accents.

In the examination, I will want to hear colour and sense the excitement; the one adjective I do not want to have to write is 'dull'!

C:3 Gounod *La Pervenche*

This should appeal to pupils who like to play a really romantic melody, with lots of warmth in the accompanying harmonies. It will need quite a large hand, as although the *legato* pedalling will hold many of the awkward intervals, it is essential that the melody is held with the fingers. If the notes are released, the weight which is required to produce a real *cantabile* will go back into the shoulder and will need to be re-applied, which usually causes vertical accents that break up the line.

It would be a good idea to play first the top and bass lines together without the harmonies, so that the simple structure can be clearly heard. Both hands must support each other in all dynamics and the inner accompanying notes should be balanced to remain unobtrusive but helpful.

The structure is quite simple — the mood and texture of the first 8 bars are repeated from bar 13, though with a wider range of accompanying notes and thicker harmonies. This is quite difficult to play as it is extremely quiet and very tender, and I think that a slightly slower tempo may help create the right atmosphere. In the section beginning in bar 21 the rhythm remains almost identical to the opening and part of its first 4 bars are repeated very sadly in the minor key. Then follows a short coda (from bar 30) which says little but swings gently over the B major tonic chord.

Rubato cannot be too exaggerated in this music and you must keep in mind that, if the piece is not going to slow down to a stop, then every *ritardando* must have a balancing onward movement to compensate. It is important to accept that this moving-on must go faster than the overall tempo, so to practise the piece at the indicated metronome speed is not sufficient if it is to sound really romantic and expressive. I am afraid this is not fully appreciated and leads to many problems in examinations.

The initial 8-bar theme should be shaped in one phrase, not in small 2-bar sections, and the slurs are thus merely small breathing spaces. Dynamics sensitively used will create this structure and you should rise slightly to the G♯ in bar 1 so that it can fall away until the *crescendo* in bars 3 and 4. There should be a slight pull-back at the end of bar 4, but move on immediately in the next bar. The second *crescendo* (bar 5), of course, should not be so strong, as it falls within a quieter section.

In the LH melody (from bar 9), move onwards at some point before the *poco ritardando*, and when the repeat of the opening occurs use the *una corda* pedal as well. The peak of this section may lie in the stronger dynamics in bars 17 and 18, but for me the real focus lies in the highest notes (the high Bs), and I feel that there can be quite a decisive pull-back in bar 16 or 19.

In the section beginning at bar 21, I think it should move on towards the top C♯ and then, to create a sadder atmosphere at the *con tristezza*, I would do the opposite, and pull it back for the 2 bars. The pulse should ebb and flow variously in the next two lines; all that matters is that it is balanced. Certainly, it must move on in bar 34, so that the final chords may slowly die away into nothing.

C:4 Heller *Nuits blanches*

Pieces by Heller are usually attractive and musical, with some underlying technical purpose. This one is no exception, and is designed to promote good chord-playing within a fairly rigid pulse.

The chords are difficult because they are spread and many are out of the normal hand-span, so lateral wrist movement must be used. It is important that the top notes of all *arpeggiando* chords are played on the beat, which means that the lower notes must be put in before the bar-line. You will notice that some chords are spread in one hand only — for instance, the first chord of the 2nd bar and that in the 9th. With these, the top note of the spread chord should be played *with* the ordinary chord so that the basic pulse is not lost. Ideally the effect of the grace-notes *plus* an ordinary chord (for example in bar 13) should be different from the spread chords, as only the grace-note is played before the beat; however, I think that candidates will play all the notes as a spread chord.

When the chord in the LH is too wide to stretch, the pedal must catch the bass note, as in bars 2, 3 and 4; only by listening very carefully will you know whether you have used it correctly. The pedalling is clearly detailed, but you may have to use it more often if the fingers cannot create the right effect. For instance, in the 1st bar you may have to lift off the minims in the RH to play the F♯ and the pedal could be used quickly to sustain the inner notes. One cannot use pedal throughout the bar, as the *staccato* notes are a special feature of the piece.

The melodic line should be played smoothly wherever it occurs. This must be achieved by the fingers, as often the pedal will be changing, and the line will therefore be broken if this alone is used. Remember to bring out the melody in the inner part in the second last line, and, of course, the dynamics in the melody must be supported throughout.

The overall structure is very straightforward: 4 + 4 + 8 bars in both sections. The 8-bar phrase can be unified by a general *crescendo* rising to the 6th bar and dying away in the 7th and 8th.